I0141877

Happy to be God's Lapdog

Bill Dickson

Illustrations
Nike Meyer

ISBN-13: 978-0692026687

ISBN-10: 0692026681

Forward...

Thank you for taking the time to read what is tantamount to a dissertation or thesis on the topic of life purpose and methods to achieve insight on such. My hope is that this book will give you a new perspective on the relationship between God's divine plan and man's struggle for significance.

"Love must be sincere. Hate what is evil; cling
to what is good. Be devoted to one another in
brotherly love. Honor one another above your-
selves. Never be lacking in zeal, but keep
your spiritual fervor, serving the Lord. Be
joyful in hope, patient in affliction, faithful
in prayer. Share with God's people who are
in need. Practice hospitality."

~ Romans 12:9-13

Table of Contents

After forty-nine years on this planet my life long quest and that of all mankind has found resolution. That's right, you and I can relax now. There is no more need for endless pondering, angst and worry. No more time wasted on what should have been, what is to come, what should be done, what others think or how I will be provided for. You see... I have had a revelation. This, as you may have guessed by now, is my answer to the big question. The eternal question of man, that is, why am I here? Why did God (of course I am assuming the existence of God and will discuss that evidence in another chapter) create? Before I answer that question for you, some background on me, the human...

Bill Dickson.

1

The Revelation

Forty-nine years ago in a little town named Berlin, on Maryland's Eastern Shore, USA, I was born. The physical me, human me came into being. My mother Shirley, a hard working God loving, family oriented, protestant Christian and my father John, a good soul, hard working, determined yet fragile ego of a man, had joined some nine months prior to assist in bringing about the physical me. (I say assist because I believe that the life force of God is present in every occurrence of the materialization of spirit)

Not so different was I than any boy born into a world of fear, confusion, pain. and joy. My twin brother, Brian was a little heavier than me at birth and I was meek at 4 pounds, 15 ounces. I was placed in an incubator to "finish cooking". I have come to believe in divine plan, even with its seemingly difficult irreconcilable issues with free will and the problem of evil. I will leave that discussion to another chapter or book entirely. It is no coincidence that my twin bore the name Brian. The name Brian means strength and he has always been strong in spirit and feisty. His cry was loud and he has always been determined. My name, William means protector and that role is most comfortable to me and has been all my life.

I have also always been a daydreamer, a thinker, and seeker of knowledge. As all children are, beginning about age three, I was full of questions of why. They say things like, "Mommy/Daddy why is there a sun? Where does the rain come from? How big is the sun? Why can't we see God? Where is God? Why can't dogs talk?" This is but a very short list of the questions we ask.

One of my strongest first memories is of my first grade year. I was, for the first time in my life, alone. Brian and I had always been together, and there I was now, without him. My teacher, Mrs. Stevens was without a doubt an angel, sent by God, as I am sure most first grade teachers are. As I cried feeling alone, Mrs. Stevens took me under her wing and showered me with attention and support. She was beautiful and I was interested in what she had to say. There were times I remember though, when she would say to me, as I gazed out the window, "stop daydreaming now and get your work done." Schoolwork was easy for me and so required little attention. I have to say she was my first "puppy love".

A few years later, when I was nine, my father's alcoholism was out of control and my mother and father divorced. My mother now had four boys to raise on her own. We had been living in the house down the lane from my maternal grandparents on an acre of land given to Mom and Dad by them. The divorce forced the sale of the house and Mom and us boys moved into a mobile home behind my grandparents' house. We moved again many times for reasons unknown to me except Mom's independence and rent situations.

Middle school brought some new order to our previously chaotic existence. Brian and I quickly realized that we had a great deal of talent in music and this became a very strong part of our identity. Our guitar teacher was just the kind of man that we needed in our lives. He was a mentor and his encouragement was very welcomed. I began to write songs, a new extension of my dreamer personality. My songs were some of the typical boy/girl crush stuff, but also about having goals and dreams and I found myself concerned with philosophical ideas and the human condition. Our teacher, Mr. Purnell or just plain "Purnell", as he was referred to by his students, transferred to the high school. He was then able to continue with his select students. One of the other students became Brian's and my good friend. He was cool and was one year older than us and ahead of us in his guitar playing abilities. His name was Dana and the three of us plus a drummer formed a new band. Dana owned the sound system for the band so we rehearsed at his house. There came a time when Dana's home life was not so good and he became the ward of a man named Ray who was the deputy state's attorney for Worcester County MD. As a result, it was Ray's house that became the rehearsal place now.

Brian and I got to know Ray very well and he was the next mentor and most influential male role model that we had. For me especially, Ray was and still is my greatest mentor. In Ray's world there was a can do attitude that was foreign to me. Coming from a home were we had very little means, this was very inspiring to me and a new sense of hope and belief in myself was nurtured. Before I met Ray, I was on a path to be a plumber like my father. I had been on the vocational track. The idea of being a local, hard working, struggling to make ends meet simple man was sort of pre-programmed. Ray's plan for me was a different one and not going to college was not an option. Ray's words held much weight and so college was the new path for me, and the study of music, philosophy and sociology is where I thrived.

These subjects fueled my song writing and to date 5 CDs are the result of that as well as this book and 2 others still in the works. My music is in the folk/rock, adult contemporary/pop rock category. My first CD, "In Time" was voted Best Christian Rock Album of the year, in 1996 by Music Monthly Magazine in Baltimore, MD. An underlying theme runs through the body of my work. It is the relationship between God and Man. Sure, many other subjects are discussed, but I return to this theme often.

The background I have given on me is of course very much an overview and this book is not meant to be an autobiography. So, let us return now to the purpose for this book. It is to make sense of the ever-pervasive question of - Why? Why did God create man? Why are we here? The answer is – I believe – in it's most basic form is that God NEEDED to create something outside of himself to love and to be loved by. And so as the title of this book states, I am – Happy To Be God's Lapdog.

A Lapdog...
Really?!!!

It is appropriate for me to define what I mean by Lapdog here. Most readers will be offended by being reduced to a dog and even more so, a Lapdog. Merriam-Webster says the definition of Lapdog is:

1 : a small dog that may be held in the lap

2 : a servile dependent or follower

The word itself brings to mind a sleepy little dachshund, a perky miniature poodle, a yippy Yorkshire terrier or a fluffy Shih Tzu. Any number of breeds would qualify. This simple notion is not so simple and you will understand as I explain.

First, why is it that people get Lapdogs, or any pet for that matter? People get pets to have something to love and that will love them unconditionally. Pets serve us as objects and outlets for our love. Just as we need (and I mean need in the most strict meaning of the word) objects, living beings in which to place our love, so too - does God. The Bible says we are made in God's Image. And so in His image, we share His attributes, needs and desires. The concept of man being God's Lapdog came to me on the heels of my lowest point in my human existence.

After 22 years of marriage, I was blown away when my wife said our marriage was over. I was devastated. The circumstances that led to my divorce are of little matter for the purposes of this book and I have, since this revelation, moved on and have a much healthier relationship with my "ex" now. At moments such as these in the lives of human beings, often our faith in God is shaken and sometimes even destroyed altogether. My faith was not, thankfully. It somehow seemed to make even more sense of the concept of divine plan than I had ever witnessed prior.

Before I came to believe in God's hand in this divorce, I was lost. I had been married for half of my life. In essence all of my adult life had been shared with this woman, my partner, my anchor, my friend and my lover. All that seemed to be real in my life was no more, and my uneasy spirit was flailing about, trying to latch onto something, anything to define me. Before this, I was at peace, confident, and master of my world. My work made sense, my decision to be Mr. Mom by day and a musician/recording engineer by night made sense, my decision to put other things, personal dreams aside to devote time to raising the children made sense. But now, it did not. All was lost, the dream of a lifetime marriage, a family unit that was impenetrable had become weak now. The world seemed to be a cruel place. I was in a hole of self-pity, anguish and despair. The unending question of "why me?" echoed in my mind.

I then began searching for a replacement for my loss. Being that I am self employed and had little interaction with single women, I turned to online dating. I was wanting right away to find a replacement for my wife, the missing piece of me, I was an easy target for scam artists and found many dishonest people posing as women who were "looking for their true love, soul mate and better half". After getting through that phase, luckily with-out loosing my shirt or ending up in jail or worse, I decided not to rush into a new relationship and to focus on my work and God would provide for me the person or persons I was to meet.

This idea, revelation, or epiphany came to me as I was driving on vacation with my little black dachshund. My revelation/theory was/is this:

God needs us in order to have order. It was not a whimsical thing for God to create man, it was a necessary deed. Furthermore, it was not to satisfy ego. Man was not created to be the worshiper he was created to be God's treasured companion. The Bible tells us that man was created in the image of God. This theory of mine is akin to the Big Bang Theory. I believe God's own love

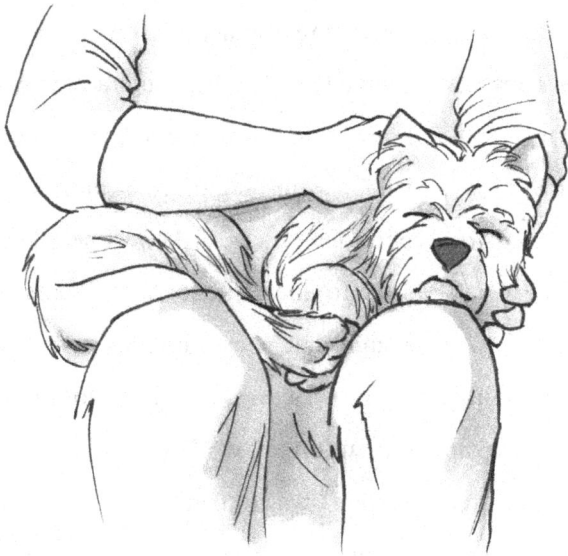

"May the Lord of peace himself give you peace at all times
and in every way. The Lord be with all of you."
~ 2 Thes 3:16

became so overwhelming to him that it was necessary for him to divide himself into the material world. He allowed himself to be expanded and among his expansion he created man. For those of us that have experienced love, as I am sure all of us have at one time, we know that it can be all encompassing. We cannot contain it within ourselves. It is a pure and raw emotion that needs to be channeled in order to be experienced - hence, the idea of man as God's Lapdog. Many readers will be offended by this notion. Surely Man is more than a dog.

Let us return to my definition of Lapdog. I am simply stating that in our initial creation we are intended to be an object of God's love. A Lapdog is a living being that satisfies the need of us humans to care for something. A dog is dependent on a human to provide it's basic needs. It is our decision to find and take possession of a pet. We decide the breed that suits us. We decide the environment that the dog/cat or whatever pet will live in. We provide for it's every need, including food, shelter, water, safety and entertainment. This smaller than us living being is the recipient of our love, at every moment happy to see it's master, wanting only to be loved and adored by us. A dog/pet can be comforting, grounding and offers us companionship when humans are less than kind.

So, what does that say about man's role in God's design? Well, first off, it is to say that God has an unending capacity to love. He is full of love and when love has no outlet it is difficult to manage, even for God. Without a vessel to contain the love, there is chaos, confusion, and no grounding principle. Man, made in the image of God, was given dominion over all the earth.

[Whether or not you believe in the creation story is of no real matter. My theory holds for evolution as well. Let us for convenience sake, posit the creation story, you can extrapolate to evolution by attributing God to setting that in motion.]

Adam – first man, this was God's Lapdog model. Adam was given all that there was on the Earth. He was not ashamed, instead he was thankful, and admiring of his master. Adam was obedient and trusting. Like God, he too soon found the need for an object of his love and so Eve was formed. It was then that the ego of man became his downfall. Believing themselves to be deserving of the power that God wielded, they became, greedy, envious, and less humble. When Adam was trusting in God's design, power and wisdom, all of the world was paradise. There was the never ending now, and all was provided for. No pain, hardship or hunger.

So what can we learn from Adam before the fall? We can learn the value of being grateful. We can learn that obedience to a greater force brings true blessings. We can learn that the present moment is to be cherished. It is when we are in a state of being in the now that all of our needs are met. To be grateful is to be expecting of goodness to come, and honoring the goodness that is.

Let us consider what it must be like to be a Lapdog. It is morning and we rise with anticipation of food and attention from our master. Our focus is on now. We see our master with all of his/her power, majesty and unending providing nature. We know from our experience that we want for nothing. We take great comfort in knowing that soon we will be walking side by side with our master. We will be led to the world of wonder, natural and full of interest, beauty, smells, sights and sounds. We believe our master is the creator and giver of all things; for he/she leads us and commands our existence. It is by his/her guidance that we are led. His knowledge of safety, shelter, and unending supply of food is awesome to us. His language is familiar yet foreign to us. We only have limited understanding of his complexities. The simple commands we obey and do not bother to understand the intricacies of his motivations, language and knowledge.

So we walk side by side as our master leads us into the world and then safely returns us home. Home, a place that is full of bountiful delights. We are fed and full of gleeful celebration. Ravishing in all we are given. Not with fear or thoughts that this may be our last meal. No, we are just ecstatic that once again we have been blessed. We eat in delight, drink with fervor. We then rest in the comfort of home.

It sounds wonderful doesn't it? How simple. How peaceful. How fulfilling it is. You may be saying to yourself now,

"Fulfilling? More like boring to me." Understand this, although we are created for this most basic need of God, we are not simply to lay around and wait for the next meal, pat on the head or chance to relieve ourselves. Like the species dog, we are to do. Some calling of work is prescribed for each of us, to better serve the kingdom of heaven on earth.

3

C'mon Boy!
Go Get It!

So, what is your calling? What is each of our individual roles in the great divine plan that is? For most people this question is asked from the time they show interest in a particular activity. Our parents and other relatives are quick to pigeon hole our talents and encourage the activities we lean toward. Sometimes this is a true discerning of our calling and sometimes it is forced upon us by lack of self-investigation or the desires of our parents, teachers and mentors.

When my little brother Dean was born, I distinctly remember how he was quickly put on his track of being a self-determined, athletic, all boy, boy. He was the boy who at age 5 greeted his day with his toy guns, holster, backpack, surveying gear, and out into the lane he would go. Alone, he would make his adventure. Normally, with mud and crumbs from the graham cracker he had as provisions, on his face. As Dean entered school he became the athlete. He was very fast and involved in baseball, football and later wrestling and eventually earning a black belt in Tae Kwon Do. Dean was not so much the jock though, that he didn't enjoy a good book. If my twin and I weren't ragging on him about the mud on his face or his messy hair, we were giving him a hard time about reading so much. He could read a book in a day or two and enjoyed it. As he became a young adult, self-improvement, business strategies and Christian writings were the books of choice. He attended college for a short period but that wasn't moving him along fast enough and he soon became a self-made successful entrepreneur.

I would say Dean, however, is a rare case. Most people's path is not so clear and often there is an inkling of an idea about what we want to be when we grow up, but it is always subject to change. Take me for instance. Again, I was on the plumber's path. I had found a nice girl, already had a job before high school was over and with a little tug on the leash, God said, "wrong path little fella, here's some talent and a mentor to set you on the right course."

My world expanded and dreams became reality and how much more they do when we let go of total control and allow ourselves to be led.

My twin brother is another fine example of obedience to

an underlying Lapdoggish life. He was all set to be in the theater, stage directing, score writing or something along those lines was his college pursuit and he was excelling and everything seemed to be on course but God said, "You'll be a great teacher and I need you there. So, here is a distraction of marriage and a baby girl to change your mind about the theater," and so he is now an awesome music teacher, much loved by his students and community and now the chairperson of a high school performing arts department.

As we examine this notion of calling or purpose, it may surprise you, the reader, that it is a somewhat modern question. Here now in the 21st century we are faced with so much individual opportunity to choose a vocation that we enjoy that the individual often feels lost or confused. Often times we search for what will bring us the most wealth for the least amount of effort. Too many people are driven by greed or comfort rather than searching for that unique path that has been laid out for us long before we were born.

It is when we can be still, reflective and aware of the calling voice of God, that we receive the messages, clues, and little nudges to put us on our purposeful path.

There was a particular moment in 1990 when the concept of listening to our inner voice of God, became overwhelmingly distinct and resonate in me. I was leaving the campus of the University of Maryland at Baltimore County after finishing a piano lesson. I was walking to my car and it was a nice spring day. I looked up at the clouds and the universe seemed to expand. I suddenly felt connected to everything. For a moment I felt as though I could disappear into the all and the feeling of peace and rightness came over me. All at once the words and melody of my song "The Voice In Me" came to me and to this day it is a mantra for me. The lyrics to the song are:

Don't look so surprised.
You have planned it and you can't believe lies.
Once we thought it was out of our hands
And now we know that we lay the plans

The voice is with-in. It's not in what they do
You decide which you is you

I walked along the stony ground
And noticed all the peace around
I looked to the sky and saw with-in
The greatest gift of gods and men

The voice is with-in. It's not in what they say
You decide which you today

And I know it's all around
I know it's all around
I know it's all around me

Let us consider the first two lines:

> *Don't look so surprised.*
> *You have planned it and you can't believe lies.*

I am saying that we should not be surprised by the conditions in which we find ourselves. We are ultimately responsible for the nature of our reality. What we truly believe (in the most rigid sense of the word believe) is our reality. A self manifested reality. This is not the objective reality, but our own individual subjective reality. We each carry with us what is real for us. The mind, energy and life force that is God, is the objective reality. All else is limited understanding of objective reality. In the quiet moments, one may glean a glimpse of the objective reality. But for human beings, it is most often fleeting and unsustainable.

In the next two lines, I am referring to what many people call the "Let Go and Let God" slogan. To believe that we have no say or control in our present situation is, I believe, an absurdity. I write/sing, *"Once we thought it was out of our hands...And now we know that we lay the plans"*

That is to say, there are those who blame or give credit to every thing in our lives be it good or bad to God and His doing. This is a fatalistic view of our own responsibility to our happiness or life's circumstances.

When I refer to divine plan, I am speaking of the knowingness or omniscient aspect of God. For God exists in the ever present now. This concept is very hard for human beings to grasp in its entirety without feeling fatalistic. I will attempt to explain it in words here since that is all I have. Einstein, Kant and many other philosophers have put forth explanations of time and so to it, I add my humble theory. There is only Now in the mind of God. When I say God decided to create man, what I mean to say is that man exists because of Gods' knowing man exists. In the most simple description of God, imagine God to be like water, the purest of water that contains only Hydrogen (two atoms) and Oxygen (one atom) $H2O$, no other elements, gases, or pollutants. Imagine this massive unending water body now dripping a drop outside of itself (even though for God there really is no outside of self, however, I will leave that part aside now for later mind bending). This drop is you or any living thing that becomes aware of itself apart from the body of water or God. When awareness of the separate self is made to self, the drop takes on pollutants. Remember, the essence is the same but our memory of the allness becomes clouded and bombarded by the physical world. To return to the line from my song now:

> *Don't look so surprised.*
> *You have planned it and you can't believe lies.*
> *Once we thought it was out of our hands*
> *And now we know that we lay the plans.*

I am saying because we now are self aware, the direction our human existence takes is a direct result of our meditations, beliefs and desires. Our individual, subjective, physical reality exists solely as a result of our faith. Napoleon Hill describes this in his acclaimed book Think and Grow Rich. In chapter 3 of his book, Hill states:

> *"FAITH is the head chemist of the mind. When FAITH is blended with the vibration of thought, the subconscious mind instantly picks up the vibration, translates it into its spiritual equivalent, and transmits it to Infinite Intelligence, as in the case of prayer.*
>
> *The emotions of FAITH, LOVE, and SEX are the most powerful of all the major positive emotions. When the three are blended, they have the effect of "coloring" the vibration of thought in such a way that it instantly reaches the subconscious mind, where it is changed into its spiritual equivalent, the only form that induces a response from Infinite Intelligence.*
>
> *Love and faith are psychic; related to the spiritual side of man. Sex is purely biological, and related only to the physical. The mixing, or blending, of these three emotions has the effect of opening a direct line of communication between the finite, thinking mind of man, and Infinite Intelligence."*

This is the Voice In Me. The creative power of God exists within all of us. Moreover, it is the knowing power of God that is available only upon listening and meditation/prayer and faith. So like a dog, we are to be aware of the master's voice guiding us to receive all the blessings that are already there for each of us.

Let us return now to the nature and understanding of individual calling or purpose, since that is the crux of this book.

Being that we find ourselves here on earth as human beings along side other human beings in whom each possess an individual ego, we have the task of navigating through this perception of existence in cooperation with each other for the common well being or at odds with each other for the individual satisfaction of the comfort and hedonistic satisfaction of the ego.

The peace of God exists in the dance of being and allowing higher energies to thrive. By higher energies I mean those that are detached from ego. The less a being clings to ego - the closer that being is to God.

This is why all of the most revered teachers of human history are aligned with service to others and self sacrifice. To that end is your, (I am talking about you, the human being reading this book) true calling.

In what fashion or role is your service to all? What path exists already in which you are the life force to serve the egoless being of God? You know the answer because before you were here on earth you were with God, in the body, in the water. You need only to become aware of the voice of God, of the knowing of the path and your human role will be clear. Sounds easy but as you have experienced, it is not so easy.

We are given helpers to see the path clearly. Some come to us as teachers, parents, employers, students and of course, the wisdom of children, who are much closer to the being of God than adults. Over time (human time of course, since that is what we practice) we often get farther and farther from the being of God until or unless we practice being with God through prayer, meditation and listening.

Meditation and prayer are very powerful specific acts of thinking.

In a recent study done by Dr. Andrew Newberg, MD who is the Director of Research at the Myrna Brind Center for Integrative Medicine at Jefferson University Hospital and Medical College, it was shown that meditation and praying to God or what ever you name the divine creative being of all that is, the human brain is activated in the same manner that it is in conversation to other known human beings.

Dr. Newberg has studied the neuroscientific effect of religious and spiritual experiences for decades.

In a video that recently aired on "Through the Wormhole" narrated by Morgan Freeman on the TV channel Science, Dr. Newberg explains that to study the effect of meditation and prayer on the brain, he injects his subjects with a harmless radioactive dye while they are deep in prayer/meditation. The dye migrates to the parts of the brain where the blood flow is the strongest, i.e,. to the most active part of the brain.

It was shown and explained in the video that increased activity is observed in the frontal lobes and the language area of the brain. This is the part of the brain that activates during conversation, and Dr. Newberg believes that for the brain, praying to God in the Judeo-Christian tradition is similar to talking to people. "When we study Buddhist meditation where they are visualizing something, we might expect to see a change or increased activity in the visual part of the brain," Dr. Newberg said.

While observing atheists meditating or "contemplating God," Dr. Newberg did not observe any of the brain activity in the frontal lobe that he observed in religious people.

This came from an article in The Huffington Post By: Jahnabi Barooah, posted: 10/18/2012 4:25 pm EDT

There is, as I stated earlier, something uniquely powerful about praying and believing that we can communicate with something that is more knowing than us.

Our divine master is speaking to us and we have the task of focusing on "His" words of wisdom and guidance. Living here on planet Earth though, we often get distracted just as a Lapdog can be distracted by a chew toy.

4

What is Your Chew Toy?

Just as a dog occupies itself with chewing on a rawhide stick and a baby chews on a rubber ring, we occupy our idle mind with temporary self-gratifying activities. While we are young, we believe we have an unlimited amount of time to explore our desires and define ourselves as we relate to the rest of the world. Many people are not so concerned on life purpose as they are on securing a job or career that will allow them to live a financially secure life. As a perpetual day dreamer, planner and romantic, I often find myself caught up in doing mundane chores such as laundry, housework, paying bills or answering emails in order to feel as if I am accomplishing something when in fact sometimes I am putting myself farther away from my real goals like writing this book, finishing a recording project, or doing necessary work of marketing and reaching my target audience.

This is not to say one's life should be completely consumed by obtaining personal goals. It is my opinion that these chew toys, as I have referred to them, are sometimes part of the bigger picture and plan that God intends for us. When we are involved in these rather mundane activities our mind is allowed to wander a bit and we can find inspiration or little hints into the divine path that is for each of us. The task is to recognize these hints and put energy and action into fulfilling the plan.

There was a particular day in the summer of 1997 wherein I was mowing the lawn and out of this task of walking back and forth I was given the concepts and melodies of 5 songs. I had not set out to find these songs but allowed them to come to me and through the activity of mowing the lawn I was rewarded with what I believe to be divine music. I was not rewarded because I was forcing my ego's need to have a new CD. I was rewarded for letting go and seeing beauty in what was. These songs became part of the CD "In Our World", in which the title track celebrates the gift of experiencing the mentorship of Ray as I mentioned earlier.

My life has been blessed by recognizing that there are mentors who lead me in new directions to explore new talents and open my mind to prosperous thinking. It is not that I consciously seek out these mentors. They are placed in my path by divine wisdom, I am sure. Not on a conscious level but on some level,

I am paying attention to the hints and following the guidance of what I believe is God.

We can also find inspiration and purpose by seeing the beauty and potential in others. I have a friend whose "chew toy" is woodworking. He is a carpenter by trade, but his passion is in building surfboards and paddleboards. These are not just plain looking, utilitarian objects. They are pieces of art, albeit useful and well built. Upon my last visit to his home, I was so impressed and immediately my mind went to the marketability of these items. But even if he decides not to bring them to market, he and those who experience his talent receive the joy of such an endeavor.

Another person, whom I consider to be a mentor, is my mother-in-law, Betty. She is a person full of God's spirit and has shown me on numerous occasions how to just be, and how to allow the path to be made clear. Her "chew toy" is writing children's stories. These are stories with delightful and precarious squirrels as the main characters. She is a retired nurse and for the longest time has spent her retirement caring for the needs of her mother. Her mother just passed recently at the age of 106 years and these children's stories have served Betty as a healthy distraction and now offer her an opportunity to share more readily with an audience.

We all have examples of persons in our lives who show us true service to others. Most people can recall their grandmothers

"You make known to me the path of life; you will fill me with
joy in your presence, with eternal pleasures at your right hand."
~ Psalm 16:11

being those, such persons. My grandmother on my mother's side was without a doubt a testament to God's mercy and love. She and my grandfather lived in a little farmhouse with 25 acres of fields surrounding the parcel their house was on. They gave an acre to each of their five children and my grandfather, who was called Pop-Pop, worked as a carpenter.

They always had a little vegetable garden and my Mom-Mom delighted in growing flowers of all varieties around the perimeter of the house and around the property. My Pop-Pop liked to hunt for rabbits, as did his relatives and my uncles and cousins. We lived down the lane and would hear the rabbit dogs barking, as Pop-Pop would feed them or rally them out of their pen to go into the woods. Rabbit Dogs are most often if not always beagles and they are particularly bred for finding and running down rabbits. Wouldn't it be nice if it were that easy for us to identify our unique purpose?

This particular breed of dogs enjoys, what seems to be, pure happiness of spirit. They are well fed and eager to chase their game and please their masters. A wagging tail and happy bark is a normal everyday experience. Like his dogs, Pop-Pop seemed to live a content life. Although I am sure he saw his share of disappointment and frustrations, it was not easily seen. I would say his favorite "chew toy" was mowing the lawn and watching baseball. It was not until later in my life that I realized what a productive and peaceful accomplishment he was achieving in his mowing. Zen-like, he was and so too was Mom-Mom and her flowers. Both of them were experiencing the state of just being.

Probably the most well known proponent, about experiencing the state of being, who teaches and writes on this subject today, is Echart Tolle. In his book, "The Power Of Now", Tolle professes that the only moment that is true and real is the present moment. He speaks at great lengths on this subject and after reading his book I found that I had been saying "Yes, that's right," all the way through. What is true about this is that the Now is the only experiential reality that any mind can know.

For those readers who are not as familiar with this concept, I will give you a little more detail into, at least my understanding of, it.

Posit for a moment that time is in actuality a mere illusion. A human construct if you will. The farther removed one goes from our planet to deep space, the more one can understand that what we call time is a relative reality. On Earth, we measure time by dividing a reality into revolutions of the Earth in relation to our sun. So the period of time between today and tomorrow on Earth is a different measurement than it is on Jupiter, for example. The length of a day on Jupiter is 9.92496 earth hours according to Universe Today. (see: http://www.universetoday.com/15084/how-long-is-a-day-on-jupiter/)

So what is tonight on Earth is tomorrow on Jupiter. You may now argue, "but I am here, on Earth. So, today is today and tomorrow is tomorrow." I would have to agree with you that in the closed isolated, narrowly focused way, you are right. But, there is more to existence than what we perceive as a passing moment.

If you believe there is a God, then you will most likely believe he is ever present, the seer of all that is. That means that in the Great – I AM, all is. Past, present, and future exist simultaneously. So you see for God, it is always Now. And so, the closer you are to being with God, the more easily you experience the Now reality.

Some readers may be left unsatisfied at this point and grapple with the acceptance of this thought, citing Bible verses of past and future events and the validity of what is written in the Bible and human history books. Suffice it to say, this is not the book for a lengthy debate or in depth discussion about time. Remember I said, posit for a moment.

Ok, now (no pun intended) accepting this position of there being only Now, you may wonder, "so what of planning, taking action to achieve goals?"

Although, there is only Now in God's reality, we find ourselves aware that we have our perception of being, 99.9% of the time, here on the planet Earth, where time does seem to pass. We are born, do many things and then, other humans no longer recognize us existing here. Some people speak of phantasms, appearing to be the persons of those who have died, but for the most part we participate in the agreement that we exist in a linier way. And, if we act as if we have yesterday, today and tomorrow, then some organization of our activities is quite useful to us. Hence... a chew toy.

5

Obedience School

As much as we often place obedience in the category of negative reinforcement that is delineated for children, dogs, prisoners and those in the military or some echelon of ranking, most people know that obedience and discipline often produce desired results. Puppies are taught to stay, come, fetch and heel. In the same way, for us to accomplish something we must also adhere to a form of obedience training. What then is our obedience school like? It certainly isn't like the dog's school, one of being led around by leash, given clear precise demands and rewarded with biscuits or savory treats when we perform well. ...or is it? Let us examine the basic commands in obedience school and see what parallels we find.

THE STAY COMMAND:

There is a time that we must stay and be in the moment and habit of listening. This is not the same as being in the now. We are to be in the now in every moment. When the voice of God tells us to stay, it is a time of reflection, taking inventory and waiting for the voice to give us new direction.

Anyone who has had a new puppy knows that this is not an easy command for the puppy to learn. Full of energy and excitement for every stimuli that is encountered, like the new puppy, a person who has come to a decision or an inkling of a new purpose is not ready to stay. The command is given. It may come to us in any number of ways. For instance, you have an idea for a new product and at every turn in bringing the new product into reality, an obstacle arises. You may have an opportunity to speak or perform some role and you suddenly fall sick or there is bad weather or some other event that occurs to interrupt and prevent the speech, performance or whatever job or task you have planned. This interruption or prevention of moving in a certain direction is God saying "Stay". In the Stay mode there is the practice of meditation, list making, goal setting and deadlines for the immediate, near and far off future. Out of the four commands (Stay, Fetch, Come, Heel) in many ways Stay is the most difficult. We so want to get to the end, to the reward part and we are easily distracted and lured by the shiny objects that we see around us.

Someone else is suddenly making enormous headway in their career or life goals and we look at our present situation through the veil of lack, fear and haze of drudgery. The Stay mode, however can be extremely rewarding of itself and with the right attitude one can realize the unique power that the Stay mode offers.

When we find ourselves in Stay, it is best to first affirm that Stay is good, necessary and where we are meant to be at this moment. To allow, even direct ourselves to Stay first means just that. In the beginning of Stay, it is best to find a place where we can be comfortable and alone with God. We all have our special places of peace, meditation and reflection. For me it has always been the beach. For others it may be a mountain cabin, a room overlooking a pristine city, or even just your own living room or den with a fire in the fireplace, or candles lit and fragrant. whatever place you desire that will allow you to be still, centered and in a peaceful state. In this mode you should become aware of your thoughts. Paying attention to the precise thoughts running through your mind so that you can slow down the confusion and intrusion from the outside and be with your self mentally and spiritually. You should set aside a great deal of time to be in Stay. In Stay, you should not have a pressing deadline urging you to get out of Stay and do something. Stay is what you are doing and where you will be until you satisfy Stay.

Once you have arrived at yourself in the mode of Stay,

you can begin the work of Stay. The first part of the work of Stay in being grateful. We all have so many things to be grateful for and so often take our own lives for granted. When was the last time you were truly grateful for the breath you are taking, noticing the air coming in and going out. Being alive and self-aware is miraculous. We exist because some other persons, and energies came together to bring us life. Yes, our father and mother but also whatever you call God or the source of all life. There was a point in time where you became self-aware and we each must realize that it is our love and being with love that we have our existence. So, the first task of Stay, is to be grateful for being and knowing that we are.

Next, we take inventory. When taking inventory you should be careful not to rush through this. You are making a list of accomplishments and victories that you have had in pursuit of your life purpose. Not only the physical accomplishments like buying a building for your business, making X amount of money last year, or taking the vacation you always dreamed of. You should also list the mental and spiritual achievements you have had, the ones like forgiving your brother for harsh words spoken, visiting your grandmother in the nursing home, letting your staff have a bonus day off after completing a project. The list could go on and on. At some point you will know when you have completed this particular Stay inventory.

The fourth part of Stay is listing and planning what will be your first task, second task and so on when we leave Stay and receive the Fetch command. In order to list and organize actions that we will take in the next phase - Fetch, some consideration of priority needs to be satisfied.

That is to say, a parsing out of time to be in pursuit of certain goals and accomplishments. This is not fun really and can feel restricting and a lot like work, but when it is done and you can look at your immediate, short term and long term Fetch list, you will be rewarded with a sense of accomplishment just from seeing a plan before you. I work a lot with entrepreneurs who are constantly, like me, fetching after the next thing. Sometimes to the detriment of our health, family and present goals, we leave the Stay mode too soon and find ourselves accomplishing very little. This is not only for entrepreneurs though. In the same way a person who is employed by others can do a disservice to his employer and chosen career by wanting more from it than he or she sees at the present moment. To be in Stay is not to be confused with stagnation or meaninglessness. Let's take for example a nursing student who is in his or her second year of training. While she/he is learning techniques and procedures of nursing and becoming a Registered Nurse, there are tasks she/he performs as an assistant or CNA or caregiver that are of extreme value and reward. To be in Stay and give glory to God for where we are, serves humanity. This is the active mode of Stay. We can be in active Stay in relation to one or more aspects of our life and in meditative Stay in another part of our life. The meditative Stay mode is rewarding in our planning to Fetch and the active Stay mode is rewarding in our own being and serving.

Let's look at another example of active Stay. Suppose you are in a new relationship. You have been dating for let's say six months. Prior to entering the relationship, you were in meditative Stay about being in a relationship. You found a quiet moment and described for yourself what the ultimate intimate relationship would be for you, taking into consideration the following:

- *The amount of physical time you would like to give a mate.*

- *The physical characteristics you find desirable and are attracted to.*

- *The personality type you feel most comfortable with.*

- *The level of commitment you want.*

- *The responsibilities you are willing to take on for your mate.*

- *The distance you are willing to travel to support your physical time commitment.*

- *The values, religious, familial, political, financial ideas you can share, discuss or agree to disagree about.*

"Commit your work to the Lord, and your plans will be established."
~ Proverbs 16:3

And the list can go on for as specific as you deem necessary for the type of relationship you are seeking. Now that your meditative Stay mode has passed and you have been through the Fetch mode of that endeavor, you are six months in the relationship and participating in active Stay. During this active Stay period, you satisfy the being criteria that you listed in your meditative Stay mode. You celebrate and discover the fullness of the relationship as it is until you feel the call of God to Fetch a higher level in that relationship or a need to Come to God for new direction or Heel to walk with God in agreement and steadiness on the current path. In this way the active Stay is like the Heel mode. They work together when a certain goal is achieved.

THE FETCH COMMAND:

The Fetch mode is probably the easiest mode of being. At least it seems to be easy. Once we have had our fill of meditative Stay we are eager to go down the list and search out into the world for the thing, opportunity or position we are seeking. We gather information from all available sources. It is important when in the Fetch mode that we are mindful to stick to our list in a very strict fashion. If we veer off of the list and convince ourselves that attaining some additional items that "go with" the list, we often find ourselves missing the mark of our intention. A simple example of this would be going grocery shopping. It is an easy task and often done without too much time being spent in Stay making the list. Here is a simple grocery list:

- eggs
- milk
- bread
- cereal
- chicken
- broccoli
- rice
- ice tea

Now we Fetch. We get to the store, and while gathering these items we throw in some cookies for the kids, a can of beans because we can't remember if have any at home, a quart of ice cream, a pack of gum, and some pasta.

When we return home, we find that we have spent more time doing the task than we wanted to and that we have gone over our budget for the task by 30 percent. Finally we see that we already had some of the extra items in our cupboard so buying them again was not necessary. You see, even a simple variance from our meditative Stay list can lead us to a fail in our Fetch mode.

You may be saying now, "but who wants to be so rigid?" "Isn't part of living to act spontaneously?" I would agree with you that rigidity is not fun and we need spontaneity. However, there are times when strict adherence to our purpose is necessary. When we are considering obedience, as this chapter is concerned with, strict adherence is necessary.

So, when in Fetch mode, we should be strict and not vary from our list. Once we have satisfied the Fetch mode, we are ready for the call to Come.

THE COME COMMAND:

The Come mode is next after Fetch. It is the bringing back the items, position, or opportunity to God for inspection and consideration. It is not like meditative Stay where we were meditating and praying for guidance. It is a close evaluation of the gathered things we have just been shown, given or found. In the Come mode, we examine the acquired thing and see if it is serving the purpose of our master, God. Is it truly a thing that gives glory and pleases God and his plan for the extension of himself in our reality? Or have we missed the mark by acquiring a self-serving thing that only satisfies our ego selves and not humanity, the earth, nor God?

If we see that it is a good and Godly thing then we have truly satisfied the Come mode and the path so far. If we see that it is not in fact a Godly thing, we then should abandon the thing and go back to Stay mode and begin again. If the Come mode brings us to satisfaction it is time to Heel. That is walking side by side with God in this new way, with this new thing.

THE HEEL COMMAND:

The Heel mode in our obedience training is a glorious place where we are accomplished and can feel a level of graduation to a closer relationship with God in relation to the new thing. Heel and active Stay are similar in that we are in a place of being about a certain goal. In active Stay we are walking with ourselves. Seeing ourselves being in the new place and loving the new place/thing as a vibration of being with us. In Heel mode, we are walking with God in agreement about the goodness of the new thing and direction. A constant prayer of gratitude for guidance and being together in accomplishing the next phase of our life purpose. Although we know we are submissive to the force and will of God, we can find contentment in the participatory role we play in our own life purpose. Now that the obedience training for that particular thing/goal is completed the time of play, enjoyment, frivolity, and spontaneity is upon us and like a puppy that has reached a new milestone, we are in a place of joy and celebration. A little relaxed and sublime until the next obedience training begins.

6

The Calling of a Breed

Many readers are familiar with the word "calling" in the religious sense and that is exactly what I am referring to here. Obviously this book assumes God and so it also assumes purpose or calling. [Please get thee behind me Felix Unger and your breakdown of the word ASSUME. (google it, you who are too young to get the reference).] As well as there being a specific task, calling or purpose that is unique to each of us, we humans - like breeds of dogs and other living species - often find ourselves in a group or breed as well. Most people like to think of themselves as unique individuals and certainly there is something about each of us that is uniquely our own. It cannot be denied however, that we each belong to some group and so it is helpful when discerning your life purpose to recognize the highest spiritual calling of different groups or "breeds of man". Famous radio personality, Paul Harvey says it well about a particular occupation in a speech he gave in 1978:

And on the 8th day, God looked down on his planned paradise and said, "I need a caretaker." So God made a farmer.

God said, "I need somebody willing to get up before dawn, milk cows, work all day in the fields, milk cows again, eat supper and then go to town and stay past midnight at a meeting of the school board." So God made a farmer.

"I need somebody with arms strong enough to rustle a calf and yet gentle enough to deliver his own grandchild. Somebody to call hogs, tame cantankerous machinery, come home hungry, have to wait lunch until his wife's done feeding visiting ladies and tell the ladies to be sure and come back real soon -- and mean it." So God made a farmer.

God said, "I need somebody willing to sit up all night with a newborn colt. And watch it die. Then dry his eyes and say, 'Maybe next year.' I need somebody who can shape an ax handle from a persimmon sprout, shoe a horse with a hunk of car tire, who can make harness out of haywire, feed sacks and shoe scraps. And who, planting time and harvest season, will finish his forty-hour week by Tuesday noon, then, pain'n from 'tractor back,' put in another seventy-two hours." So God made a farmer.

God had to have somebody willing to ride the ruts at double speed to get the hay in ahead of the rain clouds and yet stop in mid-field and race to help when he sees the first smoke from a neighbor's place. So God made a farmer.

God said, "I need somebody strong enough to clear trees and heave bails, yet gentle enough to tame lambs and wean pigs and tend the pink-combed pullets, who will stop his mower for an hour to splint the broken leg of a meadow lark. It had to be somebody who'd plow deep and straight and not cut corners. Somebody to seed, weed, feed, breed and rake and disc and plow and plant and tie the fleece and strain the milk and replenish the self-feeder and finish a hard week's work with a five-mile drive to church.

Somebody who'd bale a family together with the soft strong bonds of sharing, who would laugh and then sigh, and then reply, with smiling eyes, when his son says he wants to spend his life 'doing what dad does.'" So God made a farmer.

This speech is very poetic and one can see the hand of God in the life of a farmer. In the same way each occupation is condoned by God and has special purpose to serve the workings of the universe and His divine plan. I mentioned already that my brother is a teacher. By being a teacher he is playing his part in God's plan. He is in that way of the breed of teachers, but in another way he is also in the breed of singers of God's praise. Being a musician, he has been called and led to serve, performing at his church and for many years was also the youth music director at church.

There is another woman that I know who owns an advertising/marketing company so in that sense she is of the breed of salespersons. She is very good at this career, but finds great value and her additional calling to be a lay speaker and youth minister at a local church.

Whether you are already in an occupation or looking for your place in the world, the first step is to recognize that there is value in every task as long as you are serving the plan of God to extend love, compassion, kindness, humility, understanding, support, and on and on ad infinitum. In cases such as mine, where one finds him or herself doing numerous things, a stream of purpose can be found to hold it all together. There is a pervasive purpose that is apparent to me in my doings and that is to show others their potential as well as to show mankind the potential and meaning in living a Godly human life. I can be providing audio & video support for a client at a seminar and feel the energy of giving with honor to the presenter when their microphones work, their videos play and I am one step ahead of the next thing they need to have a successful event. In my role as a private music teacher I can feel the being of God and His loving energy when I show a new singer how to breathe fully and "love" the notes he or she is producing. Most especially when I am performing or speaking, I feel close to God and am elevated by the words and music I believe He sings through me.

You may find yourself in the breed of bankers, lawyers, computer analysts, programmer or engineers. Whatever breed you feel you are called to, aim to honor that calling with gratitude and service to God, humanity and the world we live in.

"I appeal to you therefore, brothers, by the mercies of God, to present your bodies as a living sacrifice, holy and acceptable to God, which is your spiritual worship. Do not be conformed to this world, but be transformed by the renewal of your mind, that by testing you may discern what is the will of God, what is good and acceptable and perfect. For by the grace given to me I say to everyone among you not to think of himself more highly than he ought to think, but to think with sober judgment, each according to the measure of faith that God has assigned. For as in one body we have many members, and the members do not all have the same function, so we, though many, are one body in Christ, and individually members one of another,"

~ Romans 12:1-5

7

Keeping the Dog Off of the Furniture

Anyone who has ever had pets knows that keeping the house straight and the furniture clean is more challenging than when you do not have pets in the house. We certainly don't expect dogs and cats to clean up their fur, hair or toys because we know that they are typically unable to do so. Nor are they able to rid the house of the odors or mess associated with lounging about and eating in our home. A dog or cat who does nothing but sit around eating and waiting for the next meal will become fat and of poor health. So we encourage our pets to play, run and, as mentioned earlier, in some instances actually work like the rabbit dogs and other hunting dogs.

In the same way, God requires us to be productive and

"Walk in obedience to all that the Lord your God has commanded
you, so that you may live and prosper and prolong your days in
the land that you will possess."
~ Deuteronomy 5:33

not to dishonor the home he has provided for us. We are not to be lousy, wasteful, selfish, insolent or hedonistic. We are after all more than dogs and other pets.

We are to be companions and worshipers of the awesomeness of God, as well as the fulfillers of propagating his desires for the world.

How are we to know the desires of God? Most of you who are reading this would undoubtedly answer the Bible. Your Family Feud family would then immediately be applauding and saying "Good Answer, Good Answer!" as they turn to the board and someone like Richard Dawson or Steve Harvey shouts "Survey says…" "ding… top answer" Of course, the Bible is revered as the word of God, but so too is God's desire revealed in the scientific happenings of the universe and the natural relationships that occur in this world among other living species. Overall, the theme of love pervades the world we live in and nature expresses the caring of it's own in a supportive manner.

Our challenge in the world we live in today, most especially in the United States is to become aware of what our individual purpose is. What does God desire for me specifically to do, be, have, and give? Where does God intend for me to have my place on this Earth? What atmosphere, geographic, workplace, home environment is best suited for me to carry out my individual Godly mission? How long will it take to reach the intended master goal of my human life? What are the milestones along the way that I should be paying attention to and checking off on the road to God's master goal for me? What are the things, and who are the people, and what habits/temptations should I be wary of that will distract me or deter me from being who God intends me to be?

Being that the answers to most of life's questions come to me in song, I would like to share with you a song that was inspired by my mother, the birth of my oldest daughter and the wisdom of my grandmother in law. When Kaelee was born and Mom-mom Irene held her for the first time she said, "she brings her love with her."

What a poignant sentence/concept that is. Born from an eternal being that is pure love, we humans do bring our love with us. It is only when we turn away from love that we are less than our intended purpose. My song, "Hand Me Down Love", tells the story of my mother's love, the love that endures and continues through hand me down clothes and the love that is handed down daily from our father in heaven when we say yes, "I am ready for your love."

The love and purpose of God is not always as we imagine it should be. We surely come across challenges, brick walls, loss, and confusion. It is our task to be mindful and to use the tools and help from other people that God places in our lives to navigate and stay on His course.

This song came to me one spring day a few years ago while I was riding my bike.

"Hand Me Down Love".

Verse 1
She takes the laundry down and thinks of her children and how much she loves them. Then slowly turns around and goes to the kitchen to put away dishes.

And after a while, she'll smile as she is workin'.
And then when she's down, she'll look up to heaven, counting her blessings. 'cause

Chorus
She's got hand me down love.
Yeah, she's got hand me down love.
From above.

Verse 2
Look at that little boy.
He wears the sweater, of his big brother.
And his days are filled with joy.
He runs through the backyard and out in the corn field.

And after a while, a call from his mother to come in for supper.
And then gathered there, they'll share thier adventures while having dinner, and

Chorus 2
He's got hand me down love.
Yeah, he's got hand me down love.
From above.

Verse 3
And after a while a new baby is born.
brings her love with her.
And unto the world a plan is unfolding right here before
us, and

Chorus 3
They've got hand me down love.
Yeah, they've got hand me down love.
From above, from above, from above.

I am so grateful for my life and the amazing journey that is always unfolding. I hope this simple message and concept of being God's Lapdog, faithful servant and companion has resonated with you.

A special thank you to my dear departed dachshund, Chester, for speaking to me on that certain day when my emotions were high, full of despair and the love in my heart needed him and I know now how much God needs us.

Special Thank You to Lee Milteer for being the catalyst and encouraging me and all of her students, clients, fans and friends to speak our hearts desire and to celebrate, trust and be thankful for our lives here on this little blue planet.

Lee Milteer is the Author of Success Is An Inside Job. She is an Award-Winning, Best-Selling Author, Internationally Acclaimed Speaker, Intuitive Business Coach, and has appeared as an Expert Guest on:

●CBS NBC abc FOX Q (QVC) PBS CNN

NEWS: Lee has signed with Rainbow Ridge Books for a new BOOK to be released in 2015. Lee is also one of the Key Note Speakers for Merle Norman Cosmetics International Convention in Hawaii in May 2014. In recognition of her achievements, on the Queen Mary in Los Angeles, CA, LEE was honored for her contributions to mankind, human values, and quality of character. She was awarded the title of Dame (Lady) of the Order of the Imperial and Charitable Order of Constantine the Great and Saint Helen. This is one of the oldest Orders of Knighthood in the world. Lee Milteer also became a Best Selling Author with her book: <u>Women who Mean Business</u>. For more about Lee and other locations where you can see her speak LIVE: check out http://www.milteer.com/home

Aside from performing and hand in hand with life coaching, I am blessed to encounter other musicians and those who desire to learn music.

If you are interested in private music lessons, or songwriting sessions go to...

billdicksonmusic.com/music-lessons

One of my true joys in life is performing and speaking to audiences of any size. If you are interested in having me perform/speak at your event or venue please go to:

happytobegodslapdog.com/performancespeaking.html

Bill Dickson...*Life* Coach

In this book I have skimmed the surface of some basic steps and methods that I have found useful in recognizing God's plan for me. I have had the privilege of working one on one with clients as well as in group settings.

I thoroughly enjoy assisting others in discovering and defining their life purpose and how to reach milestones along the way. If you have enjoyed reading this book and feel you would benefit from one-on-one or group coaching, go to www.happytobeGodslapdog.com and sign up for your FREE coaching call.

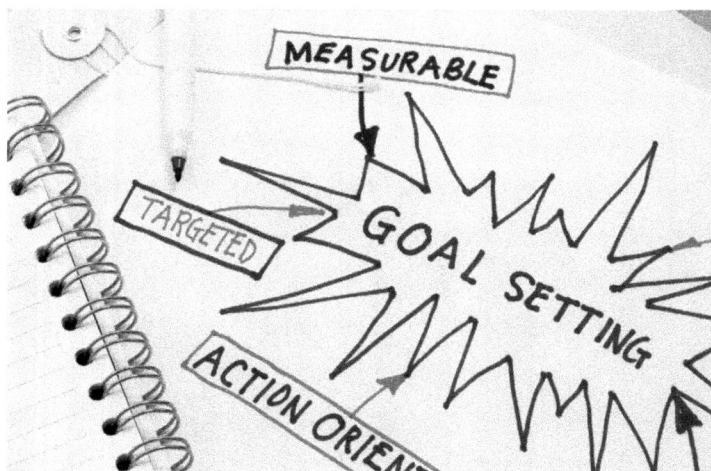

www.happytobeGodslapdog.com

www.ingramcontent.com/pod-product-compliance
Lightning Source LLC
Chambersburg PA
CBHW071022040426
42443CB00007B/897